ENTER
DARK STRANGER

ENTER
DARK STRANGER

POEMS BY WILLIAM TROWBRIDGE

The University of Arkansas Press

Fayetteville London 1989

DESIGNER: Chiquita Babb
TYPEFACE: Linotron 202 Fournier
TYPESETTER: G&S Typesetters, Inc.
PRINTER: Thomson-Shore, Inc.
BINDER: John H. Dekker & Sons, Inc.

The paper used in this publication meets the minimum require-
ments of the American National Standard for Permanence of
Paper for Printed Library Materials
Z39.48-1984. ∞

LIBRARY OF CONGRESS CATALOGING-IN-PUBLICATION DATA

Trowbridge, William, 1941–
    Enter dark stranger : poems / by William Trowbridge.
       p. cm.
    ISBN 0-938626-95-7 (alk. paper).   ISBN 0-938626-96-5
    (pbk. : alk. paper)
    I. Title.
PS3570.R66E58 1989
811'.54—dc19   88-19881
                                                         CIP

For Sue

ACKNOWLEDGMENTS

Thanks are due to the editors of the following periodicals in whose pages these poems first appeared: *The Beloit Poetry Journal:* "The Song of Iron Paul," *The Hiram Poetry Review:* "Kong Turns Critic," "Excalibur," *The Journal:* "Scorcher," *Kansas Quarterly:* "What the Snail Said," "War Baby," *The Kenyon Review:* "Late Fall Night," "Father and Son Project 22: Model Airplane Building," *The Laurel Review:* "Kong Looks Back on His Tryout with the Bears," "Having Thought Better of a Shootout, Kong Consents to Rumba Lessons," *Light Year:* "Enter Dark Stranger," "Kong Incognito," *The Louisville Review:* "Memoirs of the Frog Prince," "Video Date-A-Kong," "Cherry Bombs," *The Missouri Review:* "Sunday School Lesson from Capt. Daniel Mayhew, USAAF, Ret.," "G.I. Joe from Kokomo," *New Letters:* "Looking for Uncle Al," "Bearing Gifts," "Home Front," *Poet & Critic:* "Kong Hits the Road with Dan-Dee Carnivals, Inc.," "The Madness of Kong," "Kong Breaks a Leg at the William Morris Agency," "Kong Tries for a Mature Audience," "Kong Answers the Call for a Few Good Men," "Viet Kong," "Self Help," *Poetry:* "Walking Back," *Poetry Now:* "Drumming Behind You in the High School Band," *Prairie Schooner:* "Agnolo in Plague Time," "The Knack of Jumping," "Visiting Grandma at St. Luke's," *Tar River Poetry:* "Taking My Son to His First Day of Kindergarten," "Suppose," *Tendril:* "Plain Geometry," *Tightrope:* "Stark Weather," "Playing Possum," *Zone 3:* "My Father Cannot Draw a Man," "Children's Night at the Gentry County Fair."

My sincerest thanks also to Craig Goad, Art Homer, William Kloefkorn, Jim Simmerman, David Slater, Robert Wallace, and Miller Williams, friends who lent their time and expertise to help in the making of this book.

CONTENTS

3

ENTER
DARK STRANGER

I

STARK WEATHER

*. . . and it seem as though i could
see ny heart before ny eyes, turning
dark black with Hate of Rages, or
harhequinade, stripped from that munner
life leaving only naked being-Hate.*

Charles Starkweather

On the Great Plains in March
the wind blows for days.
Gutter pipes vibrate, shingles flap;
things begin to come loose.
Once they found old Miss Purdy
wandering at midnight on U.S. 40,
her nightgown billowing
over her spindly, blue-gray thighs.
It took three deputies to hold her down
till the doctor arrived.

On the Great Plains in March
the dry elm scrapes
at an upstairs window,
dust devils swirl and disperse
across the wide, empty fields,
and a pistol shot sounds
no louder than a screen door
slapping on a porch.

AGNOLO IN PLAGUE TIME

And so they died. And no one
could be found to bury the dead
for money or friendship. . . .

Agnolo di Tura,
a chronicler of Siena, 1348.

Invisible seeds swirled through our streets,
blown, some say, from the wicked Nile,
where dead kings sprout demons from their tongues.
Now the deep, black eggs expand
to hatch teeming through the flesh
till even holy sisters howl
for sin's rank whelp, and the dead
pile indifferently, foot to face.
Outlaws, their hour bending ripe,
harvest dark purposes in the morning sun;
the moonstruck spin nightly by the river
to glean deliverance with merry mien
as their crops rot in rioting fields;
wise men turn silently through their texts
to discover God's bountiful mercy
trapped in some untended axiom.
And I, Agnolo di Tura, called the Fat,
have covered five daughters with this fulsome sod,
which coaxes their loins to disperse and rise.

THE SONG OF IRON PAUL

from the specifications:

*1   that while serving as a guard at
     Buchenwald Kz, he did cause or
     contribute to the death or grievous
     bodily injury of numerous inmates
     by beating, shooting, strangulation,
     drowning, suffocation, and whipping.*

*2   that, according to sworn testimony
     of surviving inmate-witnesses, he
     was one of the "most dreaded and
     bestial characters" among the guards,
     "often dispensing his 'punishments'
     to the blare of martial or gypsy
     music."*

You will notice that I do not deny,
have never denied any of these acts
of which I am accused. All the things
written on those papers, I could have done.
At my trial some witnesses spoke dully,
some stood up, uncovering puckered scars,
and bayed for my hide. I believed them all.

In the schoolyard, I was called Iron Paul,
a fool's name, no doubt, but what
was I to do? When my mother and my father
left me in Silesia with my Polack aunt,
I had only the name and my father's coat.
She sang hymns in the Polack tongue
and skinned rabbits on her kitchen wall.

On winter nights, the wolves came padding
from deep in the forest and snuffled the snow
that drifted beneath my window. Their scent
seemed to rise from between the floorboards.
One morning I found a lamb by the footpath,
its private parts gnawed away,
its bowels naked and frozen to the ground.

So there was Breslau and my mad uncle, a street thug,
but a master huntsman, who clothed me like himself
and showed how a wolf, stripped of his coat,
looks as pitiful as a rabbit.
But I still had dreams of the skinned wolf,
its nails clacking on the pane,
my drained face reflecting from its eyes.

Why speak of Hitler? Where were the judges,
15,000 of them, when he tore away
the lawful state? Where were they
when Papa Eicke showed us how a hose
jammed down the gullet of an upstart
can burst his guts in thirty seconds
or thirty minutes, depending on the pressure?

And there were secrets, state secrets.
We were shown new maps of the Sudetenland
and Poland, marked like sides of mutton
ready for the butcher's saw. So how
could we resign, knowing so much?
And how could we betray the uniform?
Who would have you after such betrayal?

They were mannequins, of course, and clowns,
Himmler and the rest, poisoning themselves
like women. But how could we have guessed
after the runes and the heroic toasts
and the silver Death's Head shining on our caps?
I wore mine till the Russians took it.
Bormann, I heard, fled as a Hebrew granny.

At Buchenwald I saw soft guards gassed,
looking, when stripped, like all the rest,
sheepish, eyes wild in the sockets.
Then I knew there was only the uniform,
that and my name to keep me from feeding
the stink that clung even to my blankets.
Duty was life there, sympathy a disease.

I will tell you, I was not well-suited.
I should have gone to Koch and told him
I was a simple man, not cut out
for such work. Yes, sick with sympathy
and fear. You have seen the lampshades perhaps,
but not the unscraped flesh and not the Bitch
watching it peeled away from fat and muscle.

And the thing that's left—God, what would you
call it? My mother taught me the Commandments,
but I could not face the others glaring
at my nakedness. And, after all, Iron Paul
had volunteered, so Iron Paul stayed
to the end, vicious as a feral hound.
How they moaned when they heard my music.

Did I say Jews? There's a joke for you!
We had no special feelings toward the Jews
till orders came down to hang everything
on the Jews. Such foolishness, when one looks back.
They say Eichmann himself had Jew blood.
Oh yes, I read all about his trial, the poser,
slinking out to leave us to the Russians.

They were *soldiers,* from tunic to bone.
They were not like us; there was good order
in their camps, and they were fair: no random
selections, no flayings, no night rousts.
They gave me good wool clothes for winter.
I was a model prisoner, they said, and still am,
as you will notice in my official dossier.

SOMETHING IN THE EAST,
NOT A STAR

The old footage again: shining Aryans
poised near Moscow, taking snapshots, snoozing
under birches, oiling up their arsenal
for another field day. They mill cocky as Scouts
camped for merit badges in a lakeside park.
The water's fine. We, too, take pleasure
in what's coming. A commercial or so, and the oil
turns solid as the lake. Grins drop off
like frozen fruit, and the dead present their stony
acrobatics.

      The poor dumb bastards
left alive are herded up a road
that snakes over the horizon and stretches off
to where they put the losers. They shuffle braced
for boot or bayonet, hapless geezers going
where they're told to go. One waddles alone,
a blanket over his head, his feet wrapped
to clown-sized. When the camera moves in close,
he turns and looks as if about to say
something for the folks at home. Us, perhaps.

G.I. JOE FROM KOKOMO

*All this has given rise today
to the idea, particularly among the
veterans of the Vietnam War, that
World War II should be thought of as
a good war, a "pure" war.*

James Jones

Somehow he's become a friendly uncle: bachelor,
born storyteller, who stops in unannounced
for chitchat and a beer, who still smokes
Luckies, lights them with an agate-smooth Zippo
he's carried since Fort Sill. Forty years
ago, dizzy and quick with fear, he carried it
to Utah Beach, bent on living if he could
or dying bravely if he had to. A gangly eagle
scout in love with fair play and allegiance,
he waded past a dozen buddies already
bobbing in the surf, staggered for cover in historical
black and white till crowds pressed in
to see the fire boats plume him back from Victory.
Only now and then does he forget
and let the dead hand show, its finger
sprouting a yellow talon, hard as bone.
Twenty-one again this June, he plans
to marry, study law, then run for office.

EXCALIBUR

Tonight in tales, it gathers,
charmed and gleaming on the back lot
of Bud Price's OK Used Cars—
low, silver, fuel-injected, street-tuned,
and weighted down with the stink of death.
Two steaming weeks, they say,
in a brush-choked ravine
off Route W, thirty miles from nowhere,
the old man cooked inside,
inflating his natty English tweeds.
When they finally popped the door,
old Bud himself staggered for the trees.
Outstate interior men convened
to cut, curse, coax, and spray;
the last packed up in August,
shaking his head, advising fire.
Now, advertised only by rumor,
it awaits $300 and the chosen hand.
Boys who would wield its unearthly sweep
make plans as they listen to the dash clock
whirring steadily in the dark.

PLAIN GEOMETRY

Plot the straight line, not the curve:
snuff the prince and grab the palace.
Everything's what you deserve.

God squares him who has the nerve
to bless desire and sell the chalice;
ordain the straight line, not the curve.

Let the Campfire Girls conserve
what's left when you've finished sacking Dallas
of everything, which you deserve.

Hop on Jane, let Dick observe
you hump your heart to a horny callus
along the straight line, not the curve.

Fart fortissimo, scratch with verve;
rule your way with hoisted phallus
toward everything that you deserve.

The ditch awaits the timids' swerve:
shrivel second thoughts with malice.
Plot the straight line, not the curve.
Everything's what you deserve.

SUPPOSE

the soul's a tiny woman
who strolls out of your mouth
when it slackens in sleep,
that it's up to you
to keep her entertained,
secure, partial
to what she calls
your "personal space"
—or else she won't
come back, leaving you
to the gray boys from Mortimer
& Sons or perhaps just
some local flies. And suppose
she's already taken to staying
out till dawn to flounce
around some ectoplasmic dive
with mechanical bull
and cowboy souls wearing
Allis-Chalmers caps,
and that she comes back
blasted sometimes, kicks
the bejesus out of your
truant brain, whose future's
dim enough already,
and your teen-aged heart,
gone hypochondriac over
the big silver maple
luminous in streetlight. Yes,
suppose death's an undignified
divorce, your lawyer phoning
from Rio to say he's given
up everything for love.

SELF HELP

*"Big Deal. If I could swim as good as him,
I'd win a lot of gold medals, too."*

spectator's comment on Mark Spitz's
seventh win at the 1972 Olympics

Let's get mad, fellow losers, fellow flops,
fellow dust eaters, fellow weepers,
fellow had-a-wife-and-couldn't-keep-hers;
let's get mad and bad and high in the stirrups!
They never liked us, never gave us diddley
when we needed a break. Who the hell are *they,*
anyway? A hundred thousand softies, tops,
moping over their petit fours, worried
that the help these days is getting just too
uppity to lick a boot, or that the snowpack
at Aspen might be, well, simply intolerable.
We're billions strong, tough as dandelions,
raised on humble pie and hind tit,
and we've had a bellyful, up to our eyeballs.

Don't forget: without us, winning's
obsolete. So let's knock off the oo's
and ah's, the encores, the *Wall Street Journal.*
Let em play the Superbowl to an empty
Superdome, let the election returns read zero
to zero, let em fight the next war
by their lonesomes, with caviar and empty
Mouton Rothschild bottles. Boycott their movies,
their mouthwashes, their douche bags, their life
insurance, their grinning eight-by-ten glossies.

We'll show em what losing's like, put
the boots to em, head em off at the pass, trap em

in a box canyon, take their children hostage
and teach the little snots our primitive ways,
to say "Oh well" and "What's the use" when they
take the wrong turnoff, bobble the punt,
borrow from the guy with the two big friends
named Principal and Interest. Leave em with nothing
to fall back on but a rock and a hard place,
the devil and the deep blue sea, chaos and
old night, aces and eights, Household
Finance and the *Reader's Digest* Sweepstakes. And let
all their letters begin with, "Dear Applicant:
Thank you for letting us see your résumé" or
"Dear Customer: A good credit rating
is a serious responsibility, not a right."

We've got the bench, we've got general admission,
we've got bad stomachs, bad arches, bad
checks, bad timing, bad luck,
bad news, and the worst, the very worst
intentions. Remember "Wrong Way" Corrigan,
General Burgoyne, Harold Stassen, Pickett's
Charge, the electric spaghetti fork, Troy
Donahue, Troy, the Edsel, leisure suits,
Dynaflow, the Maginot Line, and Casey
at the bat, not to mention Uncle Sol
and his worm farm. Let's reach down
for that minus ten percent, that faulty premise,
those visions and revisions, that bush-league,
cockeyed, backfiring, two-left-footed,
shit-for-brains urge to go out there
and do something,
sort of.

SCORCHER

July, and our team's burned up
again. We watch them sweat on TV
when the cable's working. At twelve
games out, the rookie pitcher changed
his number and finally won one,
then broke his wrist. He wants to be
traded. The owner says he'll have to wait
in line. Today it got so hot
a pigeon stuck in the asphalt
outside Nora's Hair Clinique and just
stood there—waiting for cars,
maybe, hoping to get it quick
and head on. Drivers, even ones
whose air conditioners still work,
are too hot to notice birds
or children. We're running short
of water, electricity, our famous
Midwestern patience and plain-
spoken ways. Sarcasm's spread
like Asian flu. People ask you where
you learned to drive or how you got
your head so far up your ass. Gun racks
in pickups fill as if it's
deer season. Some new season may be
near. Our tornado in 1962
and our lynching in 1932 are recalled
these days with something past nostalgia
as the grass curls into browner straw
and the Johnson weed encroaches
on our suburb, where the bank
president and the doctor, both away
in Palm Springs till September,

live. The forecast for tomorrow
is 105 with a thick blue fog
of pollen and mold spores. We feel
like colonists on Mars. No one can tell us
how we wound up in a place like this.
Meanwhile our team, who's never heard
of us, sits out the All-Star Game,
which is on tonight, preempting "Dynasty."
Maybe we'll watch it anyway, maybe not.

THE KNACK OF JUMPING

In the 1968 Olympics Bob Beamon
broad jumped 29 feet 2½ inches,
nearly 2 feet farther than the
world record.

I check the wind (it's legal),
chuff a breath, shake my right leg,
then my left. I'm pumped,
wired, in the magic zone.
I'm thinking fifty feet
at least. When Beamon sailed
half a stride past the old mark
the stands went still; told the news,
he sat down on the infield
and cried. Almost the limit,
said the experts. One more inch
and stress snaps tendon
from knee to hip, metatarsals
crunch like chicken bones. Maybe
you die. Maybe you turn
inside out like the kid who pumped
his swing too hard. But today
I'm game. Because yesterday
I got the knack of jumping,
ninety percent concentration,
mostly: hold your breath just so,
your arms out from the shoulders,
run lightly, and you lift off
like Orville Wright hauling ass
across the dunes. At least I did.

And this meet's sanctioned,
regulation, kosher, except maybe
for the shorts (XLs) and the wing tip
shoes, and the fat girl who passed
me notes in seventh grade. The crowd,
too, seems wrong. Mostly kids.
Never mind. Concentrate. Find
your spot and jump for a foot beyond.

An official walks onto the runway,
holds out a red nylon vest
and some little flags. "Here,
Pops," he says, "take these
and go help at the shot put."

"Pops"? Does he mean me?
Who the hell's in charge here?

The fat girl shuffles up,
hands me a note, hot and damp
from clutching. It says,
"I never liked you."

PLAYING POSSUM

Once more I assume the position,
on my back, tiny paws curled,
mouth gaping, eyes agog.
The hound approaches, as usual,
from behind; I hear his breath,
the leaves crunching softly,
then feel him snuffle my fur.
He noses me over, and I execute
the classic flop, following through.
I hear him pace away and pause,
waiting slyly, he thinks,
for a batted eye, the outbreath.
I stifle a grin and give him nothing
as he whines to himself, trots off.
Next time I'll eat him alive.

MEMOIRS OF THE FROG PRINCE

In the old days, I was pink-colored
and taller than the whooping crane.
Visitors brought me amazing gifts,
each of which I knew I deserved:
robes pampered from rarest silk,
chargers that obeyed only my command,
would-be princesses, dark-haired
and inclined to deep, gymnastic lusts.
Tutors marvelled at my erudition,
rival coaches cheered me to the finish line,
the dying asked to touch my picture.
On summer nights, when I strolled the gardens,
I could see music, the music itself,
turning slowly through the apple trees.
All agreed that the apples dropped for me.

It is hard to say exactly when this changed,
but some began to whisper in my presence,
"How his bright eyes seem to bulge;
see how dark and swollen his cheeks are,
that paunch, that baritone hoarseness."
Then the signs grew easier to read:
I humped, shrank, turned gray-green,
and lost all interest in my offices.
Sometimes I spent whole afternoons
tonguing flies beside the reflecting pool.

And so they sent me to this fetid swamp,
where, the sole frog, I blort and leap
about in the tepid, bacterial ooze.
But mostly I imitate the leaf and log,
for the herons circle above, and below,

the water snake waits on his hunger.
At night, black things from the shallows
rustle through the grass till sunlight.

Legends tell of a princess, due any day,
but a frog survives by being hard to find,
and, in the din of night's transactions,
I have seen marsh gas glow like the moon.
And these flies are not bad, as flies go.

ENTER DARK STRANGER

In *Shane,* when Jack Palance first appears,
a stray cur takes one look and slinks away
on tiptoes, able, we understand, to recognize
something truly dark. So it seems
when we appear, crunching through the woods.
A robin cocks her head, then hops off,
ready to fly like hell and leave us the worm.
A chipmunk, peering out from his hole
beneath a maple root, crash dives
when he hears our step. The alarm spreads in a skittering
of squirrels, finches, millipedes. Imagine
a snail picking up the hems of his shell
and hauling ass for cover. He's studied carnivores,
seen the menu, noticed the escargots.

But forget Palance, who would have murdered Alabama
just for fun. Think of Karloff's monster,
full of lonely love but too hideous
to bear; or Kong, bereft with Fay Wray
shrieking in his hand: the flies circle our heads
like angry biplanes, and the ants hoist pitchforks
to march on our ankles as we watch the burgher's daughter
bob downstream in a ring of daisies.

2

KONG LOOKS BACK ON HIS TRYOUT
WITH THE BEARS

If it had worked out, I'd be on a train to Green Bay,
not crawling up this building with the air corps
on my ass. And if it weren't for love, I'd drop
this shrieking little bimbo sixty stories
and let them take me back to the exhibit,
let them teach me to rumba and do imitations.
They tried me on the offensive line, told me
to take out the right cornerback for Nagurski.
Eager to please, I wadded up the whole secondary,
then stomped the line, then the bench and locker room,
then the east end of town, to the river.
But they were not pleased: they said
I had to learn my position, become a team player.
The great father Bear himself said that,
so I tried hard to know the right numbers
and how the arrows slanted toward the little o's.
But the o's and the wet grass and the grunts
drowned out the count, and the tight little cheers
drew my arrow straight into the stands,
and the wives tasted like flowers and raw fish.
So I was put on waivers right after camp,
and here I am, panty sniffer, about to die a clown,
who once opened a hole you could drive Nebraska through.

HAVING THOUGHT BETTER OF A SHOOTOUT, KONG CONSENTS TO RUMBA LESSONS

I never claimed to have natural rhythm,
despite my instructors' smug assumptions.
"Get hot, boy; get hep," they call
as I heave onto the pattern of tiny steps
and another partner sprawls screaming
beneath my one-two-and-turn.
This time they tell me to go on,
and I try, jerking and stepping
till my head throbs and their voices grow faint
and my feet—my feet begin to find the measures
as walls crack apart and window glass
scatters across the groaning floor.
One-two-and-then-turn, two-three-and-
then. . . . They scramble for cover, shouting
"Break for lunch! Break for lunch!"
But I am now the rhythm and the melody,
tabasco-souled Latino, pelvic
with Prez Prado's "Patricia."
Coming through, you runty little bastards;
this mother's ape was born to dance!

KONG TURNS CRITIC

The man said, "He is a brilliant
special effect, given the budget
and the film technology of the thirties,
but the story is hopelessly contrived,
even allowing for the strong mythic
element." The woman said, "No,
he looks too much like a stuffed toy,
a huge piece of period kitsch,
ludicrous when he tries for tragedy."
The man shook his hair and made smoke,
insisting, "Verisimilitude is irrelevant,
as in any Gothic melodrama."
I marvelled at these mammoth words
unfolding from such little brains. I ate
the man first, then the woman, both stringy,
but then what's not these days.

THE MADNESS OF KONG

I think I see it now: they chase me
because I'm mad, and I'm mad because
they chase me. So said the doctor
when I told him I was kidnapped
from my secret island by movie men
and a tiny blonde in love with screaming,
that I was God and may still be,
that I'm immune to bombs and bullets.
He said it would be years before
I'm cured, that Mother is behind it all.
When I pinched his head, it made
a little squeak. Sometimes it's good
to be mad, if you think about it.

KONG BREAKS A LEG
AT THE WILLIAM MORRIS AGENCY

First, this one: "Peetah, Peetah, Peetah!"
said up on my toes, taking tiny steps,
with lots of shoulder. Then, eyes fluttering,
"Ah have ahlways depended on the kahndness
of stranghas." Finale with ruby slippers,
heels clicking, eyes vague, "There's no place
like home, there's no place like home,
there's no. . . ." They said these wouldn't do:
too passé, not enough oom-pa-pa, that I needed
to butch it up a little, surprise them,
go for the blockbuster, the dynamite finish.
These words stung like bullets, but I told
myself to be a trouper, to break many legs.
"Imagine you're Pearl Harbor," I said inscrutably.

KONG TRIES
FOR A MATURE AUDIENCE

is beautiful, is lover

Dino DeLaurentiis

The director told me I was a dusky
prince to fill the dreams of praying
sisters, who need much ritual before
they mate. They wear black robes,
even on their heads, and have secret
mating names. This one brought up moans
wide and deep as Mother's when the moon
swelled full. But I was not Kong.
I played "Friar Harry, the 'Pillar of Flame'
Whose Ashes Needed Nightly Hauling."
I strode to her in moonlight, bearing
a bouquet of oak trees and a bus.
This went well enough, but my pointer
would not stand. With the bright lights
and all the helpers yelling, cheering,
"Come on, big boy," I felt no tenderness,
no heart to shape the long, dark answer
to her call. "Use the Method," he said.
"You are *fire*. Think of something that gets
you real hot." I recalled the sun
burning high and gold across my forest,
how the leaves sang to it each dawn,
how it touched my eyelids when I
raised my face to make the mountains
shudder with its name: the Light, the Light.
When I cried, the sister stopped,
sat up, lit a cigarette. I stepped back,

tried to say how love grows best on ferns
and moss. "Talk's cheap," she squeaked,
looking careworn and empty-handed.
So I tossed her the bouquet and the bus.

KONG INCOGNITO

The secret is to blend in, choose neutral
colors in patterns that break up the silhouette,
and, in my case, slouch a little, avoid vertical
stripes, and wear dark glasses. Even when
everything else is right, my eyes can betray me.
And the voice, keep it high in the throat
like this: "Eeeeeee," being careful to always
say average things. For instance, when greeted,
say, "I am fine. Where are you?" or "Yes,
the weather today is free of cats and dogs.
My temperature is typical." When driving
in heavy traffic, say, "Up yours, motherfucker."
This is what average people say to one another
when a foreigner's not around and they don't
have to shoot him before asking any questions.

KONG HITS THE ROAD
WITH DAN-DEE CARNIVALS, INC.

Perhaps I was meant to travel with my kind
by caravan to Tupelo, Grand Forks, Danville,
to often say, like the famous tenors, "Make it
one for my baby and one more for the road"
and other beautifully sad conclusions. I love
the dwarves and pinheads best. Ramon, whose shoulders
bunch like a vulture's above his crooked legs,
shares his Wild Turkey with me by the funhouse
after closing time. He and I and Princess
Bianca, with the sleepy eyes and skull peaked
like a teardrop, talk and laugh beneath
the wide, indifferent tent of night. Sometimes
I perch them on my shoulders, Bianca on the left,
Ramon on the right, and we harmonize, swooning
trees with the old songs about the tenderness
of lips in small hotels. Ramon says no one
but the badly formed, the set aside, can remember
all their lives how to love. "Only death
can make *us* forget," he says, "and that's why
the rubes come to stare and why they walk away
nervous, checking purses and wallets for signs
of tampering." Then Bianca, gazing toward dawn,
will tell Ramon he's full of dwarf shit again,
up to his little moustache. Bianca says you either
claim some turf or you don't, that even a putz
like Vaughan Monroe could make you think you never
heard "Dancing in the Dark" till *he* sang it.
Kong, too, is full of dwarf shit, but he means
to wail, like Bianca and the great putz Monroe.

KONG ANSWERS THE CALL
FOR A FEW GOOD MEN

He said, if we girls thought we were men,
we had another think coming. I wished
to save my thought for later, when the phantom
lamp was lit and everyone was free
to smoke them if he had them. Our task was called
"Greasing the Slopes," though the beach was flat,
and smooth as April moss. Anyone who couldn't
grease was called a "Yellow Faggot," whose grave
would require dancing on. I'd choose something
light, a jig or tarantella, something
to go with how "Yellow Faggot" fluttered
my tongue and made me giggle almost as much
as when I sing, "If you don't mind, is that
the Chattanooga Choo-choo?" He said he wanted
to know who thought anything about this
was funny. He wondered if we didn't have a comedian
in the group, who thought this was some kind
of faggot picnic. Then, raising his little
pointed stick, he asked if the comedian wanted
to take one step forward, to confer
with him, man to man. This was our signal
to emerge from girlhood, so I raised my pointer
and tried a step that requires great risk
of self-defeat and is called "Tour Jeté."
Afterwards, a voice from beneath my heel peeped,
"Fall out! Fall out!" Reborn a man, I hoped
to have yet another think coming.

BASEBALL BEEN NOT SO GOOD
TO KONG

Who could refuse to hear a little infield
chattering to men both American and nationalistic,
to be melted in a pot where even giants
are allowed to form a team without subjection
to arrest and firing squad, where indians
play with pirates and the testiest reds
shake hands with yankees. So I thought before
I learned of strike zones: in my case,
two by thirty-seven feet of naked
bullseye. And, worse, the bat: same size
required for giants as for blue jays,
hard to grip, the drag bunt impossible.
Even the giants claimed I mocked them
when I caught three bases with my hook
slide or struck the pitcher when the umpire
told me to. BOOO, they snarled, insulting
my nickname—giants maybe in their vicious
little minds: pissants, if you ask me.

VIET KONG

Each one showed me his gold medal,
talismans from F-b-i, a name too holy
for them to say. These agents wished
to trade questions for answers, something like
the cult of "Jeopardy." "Why do you spell it
with a 'K'?" they asked. I told them I knew
the state capitals but I did not know
spelling. I asked if I could try another
category, perhaps state capitals.
They said they believed I was being smart,
which is taboo, that I could remain silent.
I take this Fbi to be a jealous god,
full of paradoxes and taboos, but perhaps
not so good on state capitals.

VIDEO DATE-A-KONG

Hi.

My name is King Kong. I once starred
in an awfully romantic movie, also called
King Kong, in which I suffered for my love
of beauty by turning into a barn door
anyone could hit. At the end,
Robert Armstrong said, "'Twas beauty killed
the beast," and Fay Wray stopped screaming
and went off with Bruce Cabot, which I
found paradoxical. I didn't know
the half of it then. You can smoke that one.

As you see, I wasn't really dead.
Neither was Bruce Cabot. This is called
"acting." It was supposed to provide
people in the Depression a reason to live.
Today this reason is called "Valium."

I have had many jobs since my stardom. Maybe
you've seen the Kong masks or the electric
vibrating objects or the new Technicolor
Kong movie. People make such things
without even telling me. This is called
"endorsements." I'm presently looking
for something with more of a future,
like being a poet or a ballroom dancer.

I feel somewhat strange, sitting
on this tiny chair while always remembering
to look straight into the camera. These lights

are very strong. My underarms have often
been more confident. It's hard to think
of any other appealing things to say.

I'm 55 years old.

I skipped college. The Depression and all.

"Name a few of your favorite TV
shows, sports, or movies try to use
body language . . ."

No. I haven't had time to discover
these names, especially since I accidentally
crushed Peoria in 1956.
Unlike the people of New York,
the people of Peoria don't forget easily.

This is a picture of my mother, the real
beauty in the family. And here's Fay
with her mouth closed and her nipples
not in the attack position. See? She's
probably a grandmother by now.

Remembering to look relaxed but sincere,
what interesting hobbies do I have?
Yes. I have a whole collection of party hats
and place mats, still in cellophane. If you're
ever in the mood to party, I'm your. . . .
Party, party, party, unless you live
in Peoria, which I already told you about.

In case you wondered, I'm not wearing
a costume. If I could take this off,
I would. It makes people run away
screaming. My ears ring all the time.

And some people then come running back
with guns. It's a shit deal, believe me,
but, of course, my luck will change soon.
This is known as "the odds."

Though I'm not getting any younger.

I can figuratively say that a second time!

Boy! Well.   Boy!

Did I tell you I was 55?

3

WAR BABY

When I was born
they had just gotten
the hang of it.
Mass production was the key,
industrial soap an unexpected bonus.
So they ashed the fields
of Auschwitz, four feet deep
around the chutes.

Busy with my new voice
and far, far away,
I never heard the cries.
The smell, like burnt chicken,
some say, diffused before
it reached me, raptly
experimenting with gravity
in a crib big as a house.

Yet those days became my Grimm
and Andersen, subliminal
and magnified from the originals:
my ogre eats whole towns,
my wicked witch puts neighborhoods
of children into her oven,
and my brave woodsman arrives
too late. When he cuts open
the wolf, he finds only mountains
of spectacles, hair, and winter coats.

HOME FRONT

It must have been '45, a backyard spring,
about the time my father's regiment moved
through Buchenwald, when hollyhocks, yellow,
white, lavender, still opened every morning
to the clatter of trash cans in the alley
sloping behind our garage, where the alley kids
waited with grudges carried like impetigo,
where the little one with the built-up sole
bloodied my nose one winter afternoon,
and again when I donned the Nazi pilot's gloves
my father shipped from Cologne with the picture
of himself sitting proud in his new moustache
that Mother said made him look like Stalin,
gloves with the smell of war, long canvas mitts
that reached above my elbows, with trigger fingers,
the sight of which should have warned **Soldier**
to any alley kid. When I finished crying,
Mother washed my face and took me to the Uptown
for Hitler ducks surprised by G.I. pigeons
and *The Fighting Sullivans*. It must have been
after that winter, in '45, when the grocer
everybody called Cousin Bob, who sold
Grapette and jaw breakers in his basement store
at the end of Cedar Street and had a gold star
hung in his front door window for a son
burned over Regensberg, would rock in his porch swing
all Sunday beside his radio and a pitcher
of "iced tea," Mother said. It had to be then,
when *Life* and *Movietone* still brought weekly news
of my father and the others driving deep
into the Reich's dark forests, that Cousin Bob,

the big pitcher sweating beside him, called me up
on his porch and told me this: if you walk down
alone by the Jewish cemetery near nightfall,
just before the crickets start, you can hear
the old rabbis in their long gray beards
snoring away. "They go, 'Jeeeeeeeewwwwww,'"
he said, and burst out laughing.

SUNDAY SCHOOL LESSON
FROM CAPT. DANIEL MAYHEW,
USAAF, RET.

Big voiced, G.I. husky, he strained
his civies at the shoulders—a man
too broad for the stuff our fathers wore.
He let Moses rattle on and Job contemplate
the new boil on his forehead. In their place,
he gave us Schweinfurt, Regensburg, Ploesti:
Dekker's crew bailing out, one by one,
till five were counted, the other five
augering in on one wing and a black
smear of burning fuel. On the day
he had to jump, the blow of sky ripped
off a glove with his wedding ring inside:
"A kind of prophecy," he said, smiling.

We, his puppy crew, saw it fall,
put ourselves, our desks in the ready room
before dawn, getting briefed for the day's
high chase across the Rhine, knowing
it would always be the other guy, the loner,
bed-wetter from Detroit, or was it Trenton?

—all this till the day his big hands
began to shake, the amazing tears welled,
and he stood up, saying, "We're having
fun, aren't we, you silly little shits."

The next Sunday, Miss Branson read to us
of Lot, God's grief, and the burning cities.

CHERRY BOMBS

The red red seeds of anarchy and blitz,
so quick, so blunt, so right to boys
who dreamed of fuse and detonation,
they came, one-fifth stick of dynamite,
veiled in oriental understatement: "Light
fuse and step back." Just a step
and our ears howled for half an hour,
our faces puckered numb. We learned
to toss them quick—on Suzie's lawn,
under love cars by the lake, weighted
into swimming pools, where beauties
bobbed up flushed and muscle boys
felt testicles retract like snails' horns.
"You little pricks wanna step out
to the parking lot," they snarled.
"BLAM," we answered, "BLAM, BLAM, BLAM!"

DRUMMING BEHIND YOU
IN THE HIGH SCHOOL BAND

Rehearsing in street clothes after school,
we measured off the football field
in the spice and chill of early fall.
Through roll-off, counterpoint, and turn,
by the grunt and pop of blocking drill,
I marked the cadence of switching hips
no martial air could ever hold.
How left was left, how right was right!
We had a rhythm all our own
and made them march to it, slowing "The Stars
and Stripes Forever" as the sun stretched
our shadows toward the rising moon
and my heart kept stepping on my heels.

TAKING MY SON TO HIS FIRST
DAY OF KINDERGARTEN

As the eight o'clock bell spills
its racket into this mild September,
it is I, not he, who hesitates
in the clamor toward the open doors,
who spots the little ruffian throwing rocks
at the Trash-Master by the swings,
who shyly searches for Room 106,
where Miss Wynn waits with the name tags.

The halls still gust and flow
with the rush of new dresses, the scent
of denim and sharpened pencils.
Eighth-graders arrange themselves
in groups to tower in their nonchalance,
eyeing each other like sprinters at the blocks.

Near 106, a bulletin board
declares "The Season of Changes"
above a paper grove of sugar maples.
He pulls me on, then runs ahead,
fearless, blameless, gone.

WHAT THE SNAIL SAID

And so it's finally happened,
in the backyard, by the sandpile:
the squeal of discovery, the cupped hands
opening to reveal something alive,
a small gray snail, a reluctant charge
he vows he'll foster to celebrity.
Nut he calls him, this ancient sluggard,
at home on carrion and compost piles,
a gloomy ambassador from Gastropoedia
with his coiled, decay-stained shell
and brain too slack to grasp
even one of the shining plans
arrayed before him: a gallon jar
crammed with fresh grass, thrills on the swing,
bright conversation above the night light,
and a halo of doting, parental love.

All this must run its numbing course.
Nut may be long dead inside his shell
before the master senses something lost;
there will likely be no burst of sorrow,
but only a slow and private knowing.

VISITING GRANDMA AT ST. LUKE'S

The Bible you asked for lies untouched
by the soft lunch and foil-potted violets.
As you wake, I am the Angel of Death.
I see it in your shocked eyes, the way you
claw the bed sheets and try to come up
running. He has had to chase you down
each afternoon, when you leap suddenly
from your bed and flee through the hall,
past the nurses' desk, out the glass doors
and across a wheat field; getting smaller
and lighter and faster, your pink feet
finding your parents' house on Main,
where you walked trails among the ragweed
and robins in the vacant lot next door,
staying till your father called and called
from behind the shadows.

                You are back now
in this bed, and the waking's almost done.
This is your room, this is your son's boy,
that is your gray hand on the blanket,
our gray shadow by the door.

THE CLOEPFULS

Gray-fleshed, mute as bluffs, they lumber in
on Fridays from the county's bowels to Hy-Vee
or Safeway, seeking what traps and gardens
can't provide—Hostess, Red Man, Pepsi,
Bud—Pa in undershirt and overalls,
harelip and plastic leg; moustached
Ma straining a bolt of muslin, her ankles
wrapped like a fullback's; Junior busy with his rash.

The ghosts of their odor browse in Candy, Cereals,
Soft Drinks, Magazines as they search
the mirror-finished aisles, reading labels,
perhaps, or simply spotting emblems: the Roach
Motel, the toppered peanut, the use-me smiles
of Little Debbie and the Clabber Girl. They clash
with the pace and polish here, ignoring the files
of dark glances to check the tab, pay cash.

LOOKING FOR UNCLE AL

All that's left of our family bachelor,
finished before my birth, is a snapshot
found in a shoe box after Grandma died:
Al, portly in coveralls and porkpie,
face like a Brueghel harvester,
hooking up a hose to water the beans
or drown some moles. It is neither
summer nor winter. He drifts
upon this household chore, last things
perhaps the last thing he had
in mind. Allowed to plan, he might
have worn a suit and sat composed
on one of Grandma's Thespian chairs,
left hand at left knee, right thumb
hooked in watch pocket, eyes
a little sad, set on high plains
well beyond camera and flash. Or
he might have sported ball cap
and Slugger for a grin into the sun
while stroking avuncular flies to Dad.
Or was there a girl from out of town,
the two of them shy by the Model A?

Who knows? I like to think this:
had he known only a moment before
the shutter flexed, we would see him,
like a fugitive, porkpie hiding
face, great hand blurred and groping
for the lens as the gray official van
idles somewhere discreetly out of sight.

CHILDREN'S NIGHT
AT THE GENTRY COUNTY FAIR

He rides the loops within the wheels
on the Tilt-A-Whirl, Devil's Teacup,
Octopus—lifted on streaks of light
and the warm, thick August air
—calling for more speed, more
spin, more g's up and a sheer
floating down. I sit beside him,
erect and rigid, a straight line
lost and going limp from a glut
of root beer, the smell of pony shit,
this pandemonium of swirl and plunge.

On the Ferris wheel, I grip the bar
and his Star Wars belt, trying to hold
things down like a Baptist deacon
at the senior prom, till at last we slow.

The grit-stained attendant humps
at the lever, walleyed, half looped
from the pint of Thunderbird in his pocket
and the rolling hills between here and Waco.
A large tattoo winds clear around
his neck: a blue log chain
with one link bursting apart.
My son cheers him on. He nods.
We soar backwards into the dark.

WALKING BACK

I have no business here, a bearded stranger
circling the block, beginning to draw looks
from the man pruning his forsythia, the housewife
who calls the children in from jump rope.
Dutch elm disease has thinned the landscape,
let afternoon sunlight glare off grass and sidewalks.
Everything looks too new. Our house is green now,
with patio and lawn where tufts of rye grass
used to stall our mower till my father
took to working weekends at the office.
Even our front-yard maple's forgotten
my mark beneath thirty-five new rings.
Up the street, Skrija's grocery store
has lost its musty heart of oak
and penny candy. A neon sign announces
"Guns and Ammo" above barred windows
and a yellow metal door. Still, there's the
bump at Sixtieth and Grove—ready as ever
for the next no-hander showing off for his idea
of the girl who'd like his looks—and the blue jays
and the locusts and the tack of ripe asphalt.

Like those who stare, I wonder what I want,
whether I'm dangerous or simply need directions.
Today, hundreds, maybe thousands of us search
the old neighborhoods for clues: initials in a sidewalk,
a rusty nail pounded in a tree, a wish still floating
near the school, where a small ghost, waiting
on the last bell, rubs the shiny nickel in his pocket.

FATHER AND SON PROJECT 22: MODEL AIRPLANE BUILDING

Plastic ailerons, struts, antennae
sprawl about, fragile as hummingbird bones.
Boldface warns: **To avoid damage, tweezers
are required in handling the smaller parts.**
We break four pieces in Assemblage A,
squirt an ounce of glue on Instrument Panel,
join Tab C inseparably to Tab N, spill
Tang across a sheet of filigreed decals.
"Grrr," I say, belching up a taste of meatloaf.
"Grrrr," he replies, his new incisor bared.

Aroused, I grab a wing, bite through it,
munch thoughtfully. He snaps the tail
in two, then seizes the small gray pilot,
and chews off an arm. "Yum!" he grunts.
Coarse fur sprouts from his ears, his forehead,
as my great black snout probes the wreckage.
Our dog snuffles in, stares, whimpers out
just before the rampage. We claw, bite,
tear, crush the rest to bloody scrap.

He nips at my ear, asking for more;
I snort, cuff him gently across the rug.
Refreshed on frenzy, Papa and Baby sniff
the air, lumber off toward the kitchen.

WATCHING THE NETWORK NEWS

My son squeezes into the big chair with me,
his body hot from digging in the back yard,
where China draws near as Elm Street. The news
is old: murder in Beirut, Afghanistan, Omaha,
voiced over a blackened street, where a figure,
small and once distinct, swells by the curb.

We watch the promenade of bodies, fires,
senators, denture wearers, floods, and touchdowns,
his face neutral as a judge's, his hand on mine.
I think of explanations: why we can't
stop killing, where the "free world" is,
why our teeth drop out, why I drink more
before dinner than I used to. "That's the news,"
smiles the anchor man. "Good evening."

My son gets up to wash. I spread my knees,
drink up. Soon we'll need two chairs.

MY FATHER CANNOT
DRAW A MAN

On the paper he shoves across the desk
sprawl three figures, three attempts
—two, really. One slopes off
to the left, sprouting a bowler
from its funhouse head. Beside it
squirms an eyeless chameleon
with two tails. The last is a hard
wavy line.

       The doctor studies them,
jots some notes beneath, clears
his throat. Trauma, he explains,
can make the brain lose track
of the place the body occupies,
of the borders and crosswalks between
where you are and where you're not
till every street leads back
to the same vacant lot. Many
can adjust, he says, but you must watch
such patients. They can wander off,
step out to get the mail and disappear
with hardly a trace.

       My father and I
watch a man rise from the paper
and wander off toward evening traffic,
outline unsteady, sloping left,
no shoes, baggy slacks, his hat
too large. Lights flow up the street
before him. My mother stands
at a crosswalk down the block,

where the light blinks *"wait, wait."*
When he steps off the curb, cars
glide through him. He takes on
their colors, or they take his on.
Hurrying into the rush, he leaves
a hard wavy line.

CONTEMPLATING MIDDLE AGE
AFTER SURGERY

Gall bladder shelved downstairs among the other
specimens, I prop up for an afternoon of dozing off
and pissing in a plastic jug, a raw draftee
in the army of the aging, who feels more like a child
kept home from school, my playmates hard at their
blackboards. "What walks on four legs, then on two,
then on three?" asks the Sphinx. "Up yours, Teach,"
I answer, recalling friends, smarter, nicer,
younger, who took their last step years ago:
one at his mailbox, one at a party in his honor,
one before he shrank for months in a bed
like this and died at thirty-five. I'm
forty-five, an age I can recall my father
being when he took me to see *Battleground*
and spent the night back in a frozen foxhole.

Still, I'm the youngest in this ward
of weary veterans lounging while they can:
the jumpy college kid, about to freeze up
from the first assault, picturing a scene in which
my father, back in that helmet I used to try on
every year, steps from his fog-banked room
in Sunset Palms and hunkers down beside me
to explain that *everybody's* scared, then shares
a Lucky as we fan out toward another hill.

BEARING GIFTS

In the post office lobby, his evening haunt
at freezing or below, he hunkers by the trash can
in the corner, eyes white against his charcoal
face, cap and coveralls fouled to a tarry
stiffness. The smell of mildew, shit, and rancor
greets us at the doors and clings like a family
grudge as we line up for the last truckload
going out of town. He stares us in,
one by one, to where we wait with our assortments
ready for the proper postage. Soon, we'll return
to the kids and ribbons, our carols of nutmeg, sage,
and bourbon. He knows us all by now, for years
has watched us make our rounds from home to office,
church to mall. If you pass too close, he spits.
And always that stare: secretive and disapproving,
like the squirrel's when he spots you looming near his pulpit.

Some blame liquor, some the war,
but maybe it wasn't anything big or clear:
maybe on a night like this, for no reason
you could put your finger on, he found himself
one grasp from letting go, and, looking back
at his freshly shoveled walks, the Douglas fir
twinkling in his picture window, that snowman,
he said, "What the hell. Why not," and opened
the hand, let his mind tumble down its own
steep bluff to a plain of curbs and doorways.

But that was him, not us. Outside,
the snow floats down, contained in cones of light;

I long to pick one up and shake it, watch
the flakes swirl about the shoppers and the passing
cars till they vanish in a thick white blaze
but then return, like April, good as new.

The line advances, indulged beneath the mug shots
on the wall. Feeling his stare, I shift my load
of books and Christmas ties, my grip secure.

LATE FALL NIGHT

Alone on our porch swing, I hear the Future
Farmers gun their pickups around the square,
squealing tires, blaring horns, bleating
trucker love in quadrophonic, neolithic
stereo. The chilly midnight air smells
faintly of packing house and hydrocarbons.
From behind our garage, the neighbor's ring-tailed
tom yowls his urges. Later he'll respray
our front door for his pack of floozies. Even
the crickets, their green ship listing hard
to winter, play it hot as gypsies on a binge.

Above this din, waves and waves of snow geese,
bellies lighted by the town, spread out
in u's and v's and w's, calling up
and down the ranks. I watch as the calls
die out and the bellies disappear south
beyond the power plant. Our mantel clock
bongs the half hour. Addled, I try a plea:
"Take me with you!" "This is not my home," I lie.
Grounded on cats and crickets, pickups fueled
on lovers' nuts, I stand for our raunchy anthem,
full enough to steal a bike and pump
no-handed clear around the courthouse.